THE INCREDIBLE
STORY OF
CHINA'S BURIED
WARRIORS

THE INCREDIBLE STORY OF CHINA'S BURIED WARRIORS

by

Dorothy Hinshaw Patent

BENCHMARK BOOKS

MARSHALL CAVENDISH
NEW YORK

Acknowledgments

*With thanks to Alice Yao of The Field Museum in Chicago, Illinois,
and to Hwai-ling Yeh-Lewis of The Metropolitan Museum of Art
in New York City for their assistance*

Benchmark Books
Marshall Cavendish Corporation
99 White Plains Road
Tarrytown, New York 10591-9001

Copyright © 2000 by Dorothy Hinshaw Patent

Library of Congress Cataloging-in-Publication Data
Patent, Dorothy Hinshaw.
China's buried warriors / Dorothy Hinshaw Patent.
p.   cm. — (Frozen in time)
Includes bibliographical references and index.
Summary: Describes the archaeological find of thousands of life-sized terra cotta
warrior statues discovered in China, and discusses the emperor who had them created
and placed in his tomb.
ISBN 0-7614-0783-9
1. Ch'in Shih-huang, Emperor of China, 259–210 B.C.—Tomb—Juvenile literature.
2. Terra-cotta sculpture, Chinese—Ch'in-Han dynasties, 221 B.C.–220 A.D.—Juvenile
literature. 3. Shaanxi Sheng (China)—Antiquities—Juvenile literature. [1.Ch'in
Shih-huang, Emperor of China, 259–210 B.C.—Tomb. 2. China—Antiquities.]
I. Title. II. Title: China's buried warriors. III . Series:
Patent, Dorothy Hinshaw. Frozen in time.
DS747.9.C47 P38   1999   931'.04'092—dc21   99–34971   CIP   AC

Printed in Hong Kong

1 3 5 6 4 2

Photo research by Linda Sykes Picture Research, Hilton Head, SC
Book design by Carol Matsuyama

Photo Credits
Cover: Keren Su/FPG; pages 2, 30–31, 42: People's China Publishing House, Beijing,
China; pages 8–9, 55: Robert Harding; pages 10–11, 28, 53: Bridgeman Art Library;
pages 12–13: Giraudon/Art Resource; pages 15, 17, 19, 50–51: e. t. archive; page 16:
J. Jaffre/Liaison; pages 22, 41: P. Aventurier/Liaison; page 24–25: Chine Nouvelle/Liaison;
pages 32–33: Xiaoyun/Liaison, pages 34–35, 39: Liaison; page 20: Superstock; pages 37, 45,
46–47, 48: Louis Mazzatenta/National Geographic Society Image Collection

Contents

Introduction

In the 1980s I first learned of the terra-cotta warriors—a remarkable pottery army that had been found a few years earlier buried near the city of Xi'an (shee-ahn), China. The idea that thousands of life-size statues had remained hidden and unknown for more than two thousand years fascinated me. I wanted to see them for myself. So, when the opportunity came in 1998, I could hardly wait to visit the site.

Entering the enormous building that protects the area scientists call Pit 1, I came face-to-face with rows of clay warriors poised for battle. Quartets of powerful-looking warhorses wait among them. The warriors and horses are the same yellowish brown color as the mounds of earth that divide them into rows. But they are so realistically crafted that they look alive, as if they might spring to action at any moment.

How were so many thousands of statues made? What was the Chinese emperor like who commanded that they be created? And why were they made at all? After viewing the army, I was eager to find out as much as I could about these remarkable soldiers so long frozen in time.

1

DISCOVERY

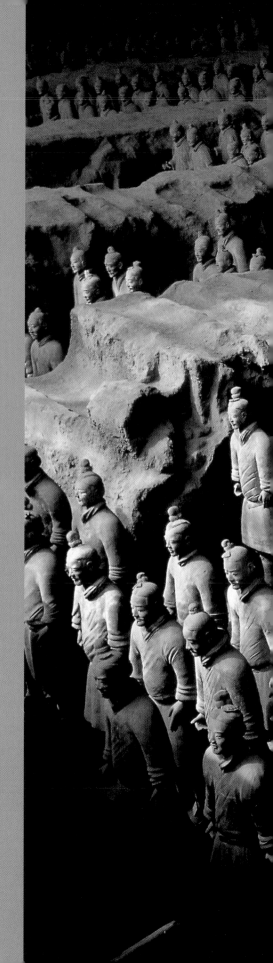

One morning in the early spring of 1974, a couple of farmers in the countryside near Xi'an, a large city in central China, decided to dig a well. As they turned over the soil, broken pieces of statues began to emerge. It wasn't the first time people in the area had found such things. Over the years bits of pottery, the heads and arms of ancient statues, and occasionally even an entire clay figure had been unearthed. Archaeologists—scientists who study the way people lived long ago—were fascinated by these findings. So when they heard about the farmers' new discovery, they were quick to investigate.

Archaeologists were filled with amazement as they unearthed thousands of life-size clay warriors. ➤

8

The archaeologists dug carefully in all directions from the site of the well. As they worked, they were astonished to find a huge underground vault filled with thousands of life-size warriors made of terra-cotta, a kind of hard-baked clay. Along with the very real-looking soldiers were many full-size horses, weapons, and the remains of wooden chariots. Three smaller pits were also found. Two of these contained more soldiers and warhorses. Altogether it was an amazing find—a gigantic army frozen in time for more than two thousand years.

An Underground Empire

The terra-cotta warriors were buried about a mile east of the tomb of China's first emperor, Qin Shihuangdi.* Shihuangdi lived in the third century B.C. The location of his tomb, under a large mound of earth that rises 250 feet (76 meters) above the surrounding plains, has been known for centuries. But no one knew that a huge army lay hidden nearby. What was it doing there?

The arrangement of the statues helped archaeologists answer that question. In the largest pit the warriors stand in rows, facing east. They look like soldiers ready to ward off an enemy attack. As the scientists excavated, or dug out, the site, they realized

*In 1979 the People's Republic of China adopted a new system for representing Chinese in English and other languages that use the Roman alphabet. In most cases, this book uses that system, known as Pinyin, to spell Chinese words. The name of China's first emperor is written as Qin Shihuangdi in Pinyin. Other versions of his name that you may see include Qin Shi Huang, Ch'in Shih Huang, and Shi Huang Ti. It is difficult to show exactly how the name is pronounced in Chinese. If you say, "Cheen Shr Hwahng Dee," you will come close.

The First Emperor's warriors stand shoulder to shoulder, poised for battle. ➤

that the clay warriors were residents of a vast underground empire. It was in fact a kingdom constructed by the emperor for his life after death. The thousands of warriors, with their weapons, horses, and chariots, were meant to protect him in his underground world for eternity.

Qin Shihuangdi must have been an extraordinary man. We remember him as the First Emperor, the powerful leader who united ancient China.

2

CHINA'S FIRST EMPEROR

When Qin Shihuangdi was born in 259 B.C., the land we know as China was divided into seven kingdoms, or states. These kingdoms were almost constantly at war. Historians refer to this time as the Warring States period.

Qin Shihuangdi became king of the state of Qin at age thirteen, when his father died. For the next nine years, his mother and an official named Lü Buwei (lue boo-way) handled government affairs. When he was twenty-two, Shihuangdi took over. A few years later he began battling the other six states. One by one he conquered them all. The bloody conflict lasted for more than nine years, and about a million and a half people lost their lives. But by 221 B.C., for the first time in history, China was a united land.

◄ *Qin Shihuangdi journeys through the countryside.*

Strength in Unity

With the help of his chief adviser, Li Su, Shihuangdi set out to change the face of his new empire. Most of the land in China was owned by wealthy nobles and tilled by poor farmers, or peasants. Shihuangdi ordered all noble families to leave their estates. They were sent to live in the Qin capital city, Xianyang (shen-yang), where the emperor could keep an eye on them. Their weapons were melted down to make twelve huge statues for the imperial palace. In this way the power of these important families was crushed, so they could not challenge the rule of the new government.

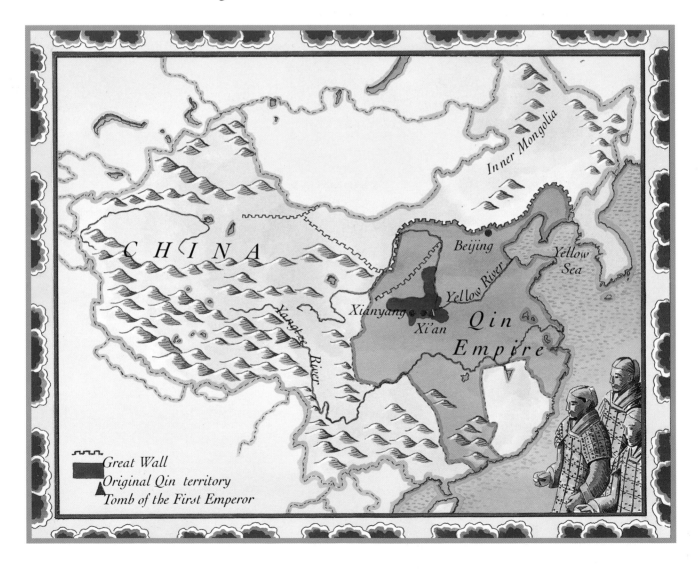

Many more changes followed. For the first time peasants were allowed to own land, as long as they paid a land tax. Everyone, rich and poor, now had to obey the law. People loyal to the emperor were rewarded. Those who disagreed with his policies were severely punished.

Qin Shihuangdi understood that in unity there is strength. Before his rule each of the seven states had its own version of the Chinese alphabet. Under the Qin dynasty one form of writing became the standard for everyone.

Shihuangdi also unified the system of weights and measures and issued a standard form of money. In the past each state had used its own money, with different values and sizes. Some types of money were awkward and hard to handle. In one state, for example, coins were shaped like a sword and could be up to six inches (fifteen centimeters) long. Under the First Emperor everyone used the same small round coins. The coins had a square hole in the center, so they could be strung together for easy counting and carrying.

An ancient Chinese form of money, in the shape of a sword

Forced to Labor

Qin Shihuangdi's policies united and strengthened China, but in accomplishing his goals, he was a harsh ruler. Those who criticized the government could be executed, along with their entire family. According to some historical accounts, the First Emperor once

Writing in Chinese

English and many other languages such as French, Spanish, and German are written using an alphabet of twenty to thirty letters. Chinese uses characters instead of letters. Each character stands for a complete idea, object, or sound. The characters grew out of the picture writing of the early Chinese people.

Many characters represent simple things, such as *eye*, *wood*, *sun*, or *water*. Others are made up of combinations of these basic characters. The character for *good*, for example, combines the symbol for *female*

with that for *son*. Most Chinese characters have two parts, or elements. One element tells something about the meaning. The other says something about how the character is pronounced.

Written Chinese is hard to learn because it has more than 40,000 characters, and each must be memorized separately. For most practical purposes only a few thousand characters are needed. An educated Chinese person knows about 3,000 characters.

In the past Chinese was written in vertical columns instead of lines across a page. The first column was at the right side of the page, so Chinese was read from right to left. Nowadays, on the Chinese mainland, most people write the way we do in the West, in lines across the page, from left to right. In Taiwan and Hong Kong, however, newspapers are still printed in the old style.

The art of fine handwriting, called calligraphy, has long been practiced in China. Along with painting and poetry, it is considered one of the "three perfections"—the three greatest forms of artistic expression. Calligraphers use a pointed brush made from animal hair. They hold the brush straight up above the page and paint the characters in graceful strokes without ever touching their hands or elbows to the paper.

The art of calligraphy requires much practice in shaping the characters to make them as beautiful and as graceful as possible.

Shihuangdi was a stern, demanding ruler.

ordered 460 scholars buried alive for daring to criticize his orders. Millions of other people were ordered to serve in the military or were condemned to forced labor for breaking minor laws. The emperor's large workforce built public projects such as palaces, walls, or roads.

The network of roads that Shihuangdi built enabled his soldiers to respond quickly to military threats. They also allowed the emperor to travel and inspect his kingdom personally. One of the roads became famous because it was so long and straight. This "straight road" ran due north for about 435 miles (702 kilometers) from Xianyang to the plains of Inner Mongolia. It was 164 feet (50 meters) wide. To make this broad road, workers leveled hills and used the soil to fill in the valleys between. Four layers of densely packed earth were placed one atop another. The soil was so well packed that trees cannot grow there even today.

Rewriting History

Despite the threat of harsh punishment, some people continued to criticize Qin Shihuangdi's policies. They wanted to bring back the old system of government, with its large estates governed by nobles. In 213 B.C. the emperor and his adviser Li Su decided to silence these critics by destroying all records of the past.

Shihuangdi ordered that all books be burned except histories of the Qin dynasty and works on practical subjects such as medicine and agriculture. Many books were lost forever, including those written by the followers of famous Chinese philosophers such as Confucius. Fortunately, brave scholars managed to hide or memorize some of the most important writings. After the end of Qin rule, these books were restored.

Qin Shihuangdi's rule lasted only a short time as history goes: thirty-six years. And four years after his death, his empire crumbled. But the First Emperor changed China forever. Under his rule the idea of one China took root. People no longer thought of themselves as members of separate tribes but as Chinese.

The First Emperor watches while books are burned and scholars killed. ➤

The Great Wall of China

One of the most famous sights in China is the Great Wall. Few tourists come to the country without visiting this amazing construction. The wall runs for 1,400 miles (2,258 kilometers) along the mountain ridges of northern China. It is up to 30 feet (9 meters) tall and so wide that its flat top was once used as a road for armies traveling from one place to another.

The Great Wall was built as a defense against tribes of nomads to the north. Rainfall in that region is often scarce and the land unfit for farming. From time to time bands of northerners raided the rich farms and cities in the heart of China. Mounted on swift horses and armed with bows, the nomads devastated homes and captured flocks of sheep and other farm animals. Even the strongest wall could not keep out every raider. But the Great Wall made it much harder for horsemen to slip into China and escape with stolen riches.

Construction of the Great Wall is often credited to the First Emperor. But in fact the first earthen barriers were built before the Qin dynasty. Qin Shihuangdi had these separate walls strengthened and added long sections to connect them.

Shihuangdi's Great Wall was made of mounded earth. In later years rulers of the Ming dynasty (A.D. 1368–1644) had the present-day brick wall constructed, using millions of laborers. The Great Wall that tourists visit today includes sections rebuilt by the modern Chinese government and stairs that have been added to the steepest sections.

The Great Wall extends across the rugged mountains as far as the eye can see. ➤

3

TO LIVE FOREVER

Qin Shihuangdi had two goals in life. The first was to unite China. The second was to live forever. He believed that he could achieve his second goal and become immortal if he could just find a substance called the elixir of life. During his reign Shihuangdi made five journeys to sacred mountains in search of that magical potion.

The Eternal City

Even as Shihuangdi searched for immortality, he was building his own tomb and underground empire. Perhaps he thought that if he could not find eternal life in the physical world, he might at least live forever in the world of the spirits.

Shihuangdi's fabulous tomb has yet to be excavated. But nearby, warriors and horses, meant to protect the great ruler in the afterlife, have been unearthed. ➤

Work on the tomb complex began shortly after the First Emperor came to power and continued throughout his rule. More than 700,000 people labored on the project, but it was still not completed by the time the emperor died thirty-six years later.

Shihuangdi's underground city is the largest known tomb complex devoted to a single ruler. From the giant mound of earth that rises above the tomb itself, the city stretches for more than nine miles (fifteen kilometers) in all directions. So far, archaeologists working at the site have uncovered the remains of a palace as well as miniature bronze chariots, perhaps intended to help the emperor's soul on its journeys after death. They have uncovered the skeletons of people, horses, and rare animals. Their most interesting find so far, however, are the pits holding the First Emperor's clay army. The largest of these pits is 775 feet (236 meters) long and 321 feet (98 meters) wide—about the size of five football fields.

The Emperor's Tomb

Archaeologists have not yet excavated the building that houses Qin Shihuangdi's body. All information about this hidden wonder comes from books written not long after the emperor's death. We know that the tomb is buried deep underground, with its bottom at least ninety-eight feet (thirty meters) below the earth's surface. To keep water from seeping in, the tomb builders coated the stone walls with melted copper, then painted them over with lacquer. Soil to cover the

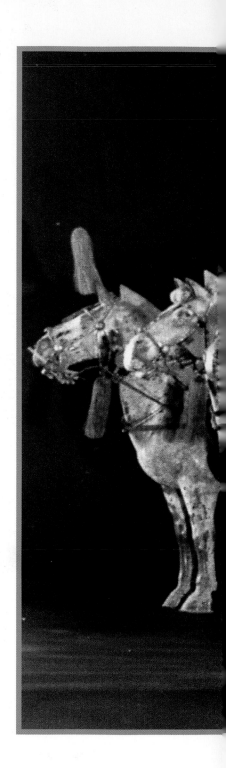

A miniature bronze chariot from the emperor's underground city

tomb was dug from a location more than a mile (1.6 kilometers) away. The hole left by the workers still remains. Today it is filled with water and serves as a reservoir.

Here is how an ancient historian named Sima Qian (sh-ma shen), writing some one hundred years after the emperor's death, described the tomb:

> *Rare treasures and jewels, removed from various palaces, towers and halls, filled the grave. Craftsmen were ordered to set arrows on crossbows, which would shoot automatically at anyone breaking in. Rivers and seas in miniature were dug and filled with mercury, made to flow by mechanical devices. On the ceiling, stars and planets were set, on the floor topographical [showing the surface of the land] features of the earth. Candles were lighted, burning fish fat, so that they might keep the grave chambers lit for a long time.*

Sima Qian reported that the emperor had temples constructed above the ground near the tomb for the worship of his departed spirit. A "hall of the spirit" was built, and Shihuangdi's crown, robe, and bedding were placed inside. Living caretakers were commanded to "make the bed, bring water and prepare the toilet articles" every day after the emperor's death, just as if he were living there.

"A Sea of Warriors"

Thousands of warrior statues stand poised for battle in the pits near the emperor's tomb, ready to protect and defend his fabulous eternal city. Shihuangdi's real army was reportedly one million strong, "a sea of warriors with the courage of tigers." The statues were meant to represent these courageous soldiers as closely as possible.

Of the thousands of clay warriors unearthed so far, no two are exactly alike. Young men eager for battle stand beside older, more thoughtful soldiers. A general calmly surveys his troops, while a broad-cheeked swordsman glares fiercely. Because each statue has its

Robbing the Dead

Are all the treasures that were placed inside Qin Shihuangdi's tomb still there, awaiting discovery by archaeologists? Or have they been stolen by grave robbers?

According to one ancient author, the people who overthrew the Qin dynasty put 300,000 men to work removing valuables from the emperor's tomb. After thirty days, this writer said, the workers still couldn't get all the treasures out.

Some archaeologists who have examined the giant mound of earth covering the emperor's tomb dispute that account. They believe that the burial mound probably hasn't been disturbed in the more than two thousand years since it was made. Further, the scientists have found that the soil in the mound contains many times the normal amount of mercury. Perhaps the miniature "rivers and seas . . . filled with mercury" described by historian Sima Qian will one day come to light, along with the other hidden wonders of the First Emperor's tomb.

own unique personality—and because they all look so lifelike—some archaeologists believe that soldiers in the emperor's living army must have posed for them.

The Qin army was made up of the tallest, strongest men in the empire. The terra-cotta warriors are tall, too. On average the figures are 5 feet, 11 inches (1.8 meters) in height. Some are as tall as 6 feet, 7 inches (2 meters)—probably taller than any of the emperor's real warriors.

Dressed for War

The faces of the statues show that the emperor's army included men from many different parts of China. Some figures have the facial features of present-day farmers from China's plains, while others look like shepherds from the country's northern grasslands. Altogether the statues represent ten different head shapes. To the Chinese, each shape indicated a different type of personality. For example, a person with a broad forehead and pointed chin was thought to be watchful and alert. Many warriors with these features are found in the front of the clay army, where a special alertness to approaching danger would be valuable.

The statues' hairstyles vary, too. Most of the warriors have long hair that is braided and gathered up into a knot on top of the head. Some wear the knots in the center of the head, others off to a side. Some have a beard or mustache, while others are clean-shaven.

Clothing styles also vary greatly. Armor capes in many different styles protect the warriors' chests, shoulders, and upper arms. In real life these armor garments were made of leather with pieces of bronze attached. Some warriors lack armor, allowing them to move quickly. The army's leaders look different from the foot soldiers. The generals wear double-layered robes with plates of armor across the chest, and the tips of their shoes turn up. While most of the lower-ranking

◄ *An archer kneels as if ready to unleash an arrow from his bow, which has been lost.*

soldiers are bareheaded, those of higher rank may wear flat caps.

In some cases clothing style has helped archaeologists identify the regions the emperor's soldiers came from. For example, the style of clothing and the skullcaps worn by the cavalrymen (soldiers who ride on horseback) indicate that these soldiers came from the lands along China's northern borders. The northern peoples were known as skilled

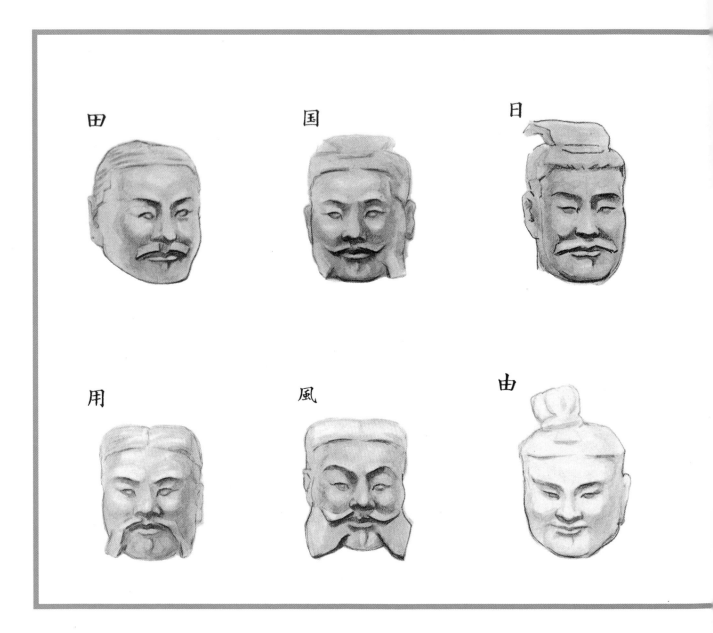

horsemen, so it is not surprising that they would be chosen to serve in the great army's cavalry.

All the many different statues, arrayed in battle formation, form a strong and balanced force, ready to face any enemy. Like the real army of Qin, the terra-cotta warriors seem well able to protect an empire.

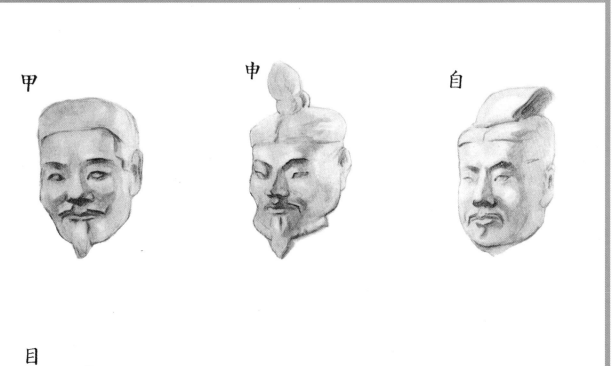

The Chinese believed that each of the ten main head shapes was associated with a different kind of personality.

Warhorses

Unlike the warriors, the horses that serve in the First Emperor's clay army are not unique individuals. More than six hundred chariot and cavalry horses have been uncovered, all with the same basic form. Each horse is life-size, at 5 feet, 8 inches (1.7 meters) tall. Each is powerfully built, with a sturdy body and strong legs. The manes are cut short and the forelocks (locks of hair on the forehead) are divided in half and brushed to the sides. The horses look alert, with heads raised and ears pricked forward.

Four chariot horses stand side by side before each chariot. Their harnesses, made of golden beads and bronze tubes, have fallen from their bodies. The cavalry horses wear blankets topped with saddles. The saddles were shaped from clay and painted in shades of red, white, brown, and blue. Each cavalry horse also has a bronze bit as well as a bridle and reins made from stone tubes strung on wires.

Before the pits were discovered, historians thought that the saddle was invented during a later dynasty. Now we know that the Qin also saddled their horses.

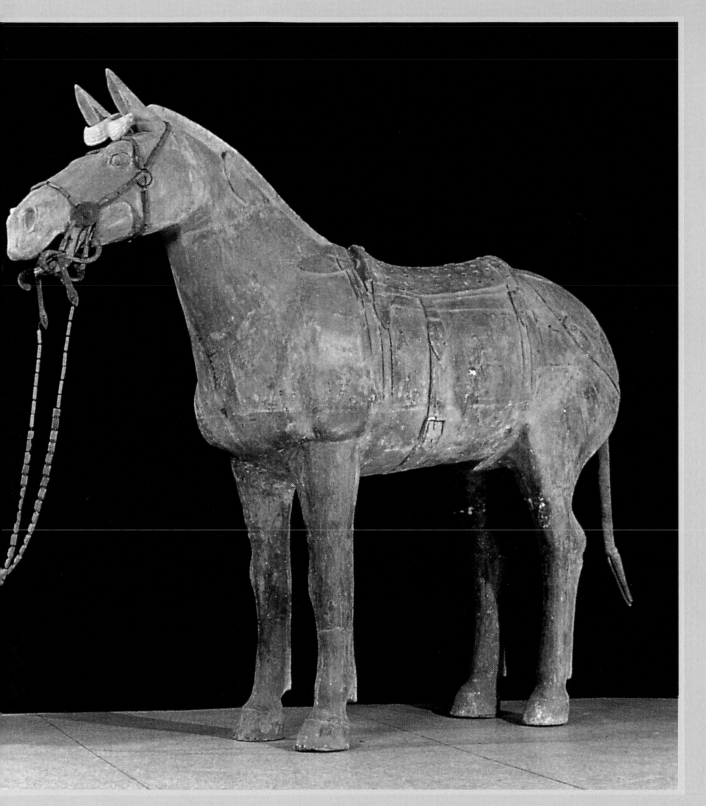

The blanket and saddle were molded in clay on the backs of the cavalry horses. The hole in the horse's side was necessary during the firing of the statue to allow hot air from inside to escape.

4

UNCOVERING AN ARMY

Since the discovery of the terra-cotta warriors in 1974, archaeologists have been carefully at work, slowly uncovering the emperor's underground city. So far, they have dug out four main areas, which they call Pit 1, Pit 2, Pit 3, and Pit 4. Each pit was originally a large brick-paved vault under the ground. The front of each faces east, the direction from which the emperor's enemies were most likely to come.

Rows of hard-packed earth separate the columns of warriors. Long wooden planks were placed across these earthen rows to make a roof. The planks were then covered with straw matting, followed by a layer of clay and soil. The top of the roofing over Pit 1 once rose about 6 feet (1.8 meters) above the ground.

◄ *Reassembling the broken statues is a very time-consuming job. Some are so badly shattered that they can't be put back together again.*

Most of the statues found in the pits were broken in many pieces. Archaeologists have been slowly putting these back together, reconstructing the arrangement of the army.

Ready for Battle

The main body of the terra-cotta army was found in the largest area, Pit 1. Archaeologists estimate that more than six thousand life-size warriors and horses fill this huge vault. Only part of it has been excavated. There are nine main columns of soldiers standing four abreast, facing east. The soldiers are grouped according to the types of weapons they carry. At the head of each column are archers carrying crossbows, along with the remains of wooden chariots. Each of the chariots is drawn by four clay horses and has a three-man team, which includes the chariot driver and two armed warriors. Along the northern, western, and southern borders of the army, archers face forward, guarding the sides and rear. This arrangement of forces represents one of the ten formations described in an ancient Chinese book on war.

So far, archaeologists have only uncovered part of Pit 2. Excavation of this area began in 1994 and continues today. Pit 2 is L-shaped and covers about 7,000 square yards (5,800 square meters), an area larger than a football field. The arrangement of the figures is the most complex of the three pits. Archers make up the front rows, with some kneeling and others standing behind them, ready to shoot arrows over their heads. In the northern part of the pit are columns of chariots, infantry (foot soldiers), and cavalry. The cavalrymen carry a bow in one hand and hold their horses' reins with the other. To the south, a large area holds sixty-four reserve chariots.

Pit 3 has been completely uncovered. This small U-shaped vault, about the size of two tennis courts, appears to be the army's command center. Positioned to the rear of the other two pits, it is well protected by their warrior forces. Inside Pit 3 are sixty-eight warriors and the elaborately decorated chariot of a commander.

Pit 4, discovered in 1977, is completely empty. Some archaeologists believe that work had just begun on this area of the underground

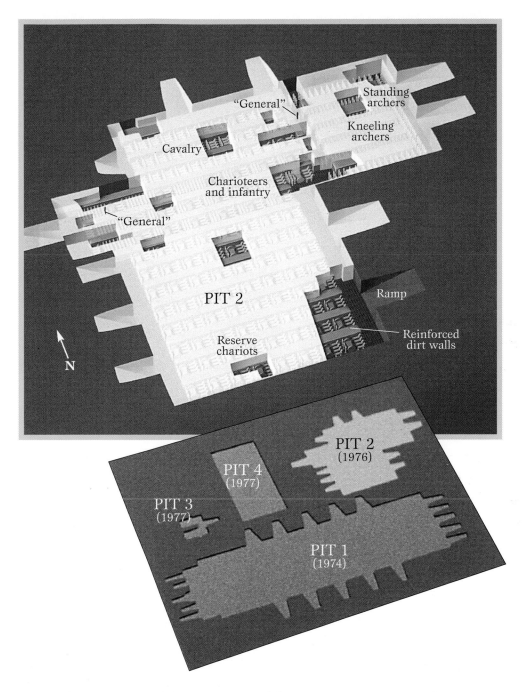

Top: *The positions of various parts of the emperor's army can be seen in Pit 2. Much of this pit has not been excavated yet.* Bottom: *Pit 1 is the largest of the underground vaults. Scientists believe it may contain more than six thousand clay warriors and horses. It, too, has not been fully uncovered.*

city when Qin Shihuangdi died. Another pit was discovered in 1997. No one yet knows what it contains.

Reconstructing the Past

Archaeologists have to be patient. They cannot simply dig in with shovels to uncover the mysteries of the past. Instead they must use delicate tools and work very slowly, uncovering a site bit by bit.

The workers at Xi'an used trowels and scrapers to remove areas of the soil covering the site. They discovered the remains of the long wooden planks that once formed the roofing of the pits, as well as traces of the straw matting that had been spread on top. Carefully removing the ancient timbers, they uncovered the underground army.

Today a museum has been built over Pits 1, 2, and 3. New buildings protect the sites and allow visitors to view the figures and watch the archaeologists at work. Excavation now is focused on Pit 2. Workers using small scrapers, bamboo sticks, fine brushes, and other delicate tools are clearing away the dirt that has been collecting for more than two thousand years. As they work, they often stop to make drawings, take photographs, and jot down notes of their discoveries.

The archaeologists carefully label everything they find. Since most of the statues are in pieces, this is no small task. The next step is putting the pieces together. Slowly the workers try to match up pieces that were found close together. "If we find one piece that fits in a day—that's a lucky day," said one worker who spent nineteen years mending broken warriors. Once a statue is re-created, it is returned to its original position in the army.

Perhaps the most difficult part of the work is reconstructing the chariots and weapons. Most of the chariots were made of wood and have disintegrated. Traces of their wheels, shafts, and other parts remain only as impressions in the earth. The wooden parts of weapons have also decayed. Archaeologists using thin bamboo sticks and tiny brushes search for the markings these weapons left in the dirt. Those markings may be as delicate as the impressions left by an arrow's long-vanished end feathers.

A worker carefully attaches the head to a statue.

Ancient Artifacts on Computer

The amount of information that archaeologists are gathering about Qin Shihuangdi's burial site is overwhelming. A few decades ago it would have been nearly impossible to organize and store all these details in a way that would allow people to easily find the facts they need. But luckily, today's computers are perfect for the job.

At a computer center in the museum that covers the pits, descriptions of every item found by excavators are entered into a computer database. Researchers who want to learn about the findings in a particular section of the site can simply call up that area. A monitor shows an image of the area and offers all kinds of other information, including videos of the site and facts about the archaeologists and the methods they used to find and restore the artifacts. It is also possible to call up photographs and sketches of each soldier and every other artifact found.

In time the museum plans to put information about the tomb complex on the World Wide Web. That will give people all around the world a close-up look at the First Emperor's ancient clay warriors.

Deadly Weapons

The emperor's clay soldiers were well equipped for warfare in the afterlife. They carried real weapons, made mainly of bronze. Archaeologists have unearthed many varieties of swords, spears, daggers, maces, and other weapons, along with arrows and parts of crossbows. The Qin crossbow was a particularly deadly weapon. Its arrows, called bolts, could pierce armor at a distance of 650 feet (198 meters).

Another weapon found in the pits, called a pi, is a kind of spear with double blades. No one had ever seen a pi before, though the weapon is mentioned in writings from the times. The pi was once thought to have a short shaft, but now we know that it actually had the longest shaft of all the weapons used by Qin warriors.

The weapons found in the pits are as uniformly made as those produced by machines today. No one knows exactly how Qin crafts-people were able to make them so strong and precise. We do know that the weapon makers protected their sword blades with a technique that was not developed in the rest of the world until modern times. They coated the bronze blades with a very thin layer of a metal called chromium. This coating protected the weapons from rust and corrosion, so that they are still bright and deadly sharp even after being buried for centuries.

The weapons of Qin Shihuangdi's army were as beautifully designed as they were deadly. The First Emperor seems to have greatly valued the artistry of his weapon makers. He also employed the most skillful potters in the empire, for they were the artists who would create the clay army that would guard him for eternity.

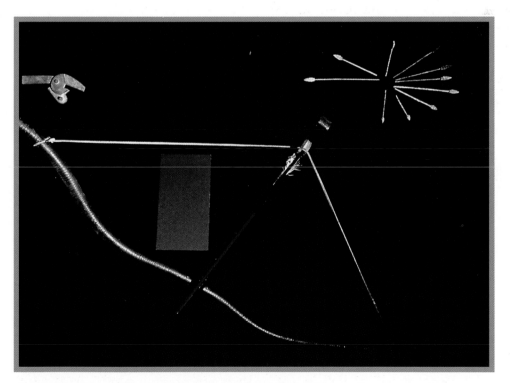

A powerful crossbow, with its arrows, restored from the excavations

5

QIN ARTISTRY

Pottery, the art of making objects from clay, is one of the oldest expressions of human creativity. Clay objects may be simply practical things or they may be great works of art. In China pottery has a long history. Chinese craftspeople began to use the potter's wheel more than a thousand years before the First Emperor was born. By the time Qin Shihuangdi began work on his underground empire, potters in China were highly skilled. The terra-cotta warriors are proof of that.

Each warrior statue is inscribed on the back with the name of the potter who made it. The names of more than eighty different craftsmen have been found so far. The potters

◄ *Clay was skillfully shaped and pinched to produce this warrior's individual face.*

had to overcome many technical problems in order to create the army. Size alone made the job difficult. Each finished statue weighs more than 400 pounds (181 kilograms). The potters had to work with the figures while the clay was wet and much heavier. All of the parts had to be carefully made and attached so that their weight would not deform the statue. The clay also had to be carefully formulated. Qin potters mixed in finely ground sand to help keep the clay from cracking during firing.

Shaping an Army

Each statue stands on a square pedestal that was formed in a mold. The feet of some of the figures were also made in the pedestal mold, while others were made separately and attached later. The legs were formed next. After they had dried slightly, the body was added.

Bodies and arms were made by what is known as the coil method, one of the oldest and simplest ways of making pottery. The clay was rolled into long strips, which the potter then coiled, or looped, one on top of another. Placing a hand inside the body to support the clay, the worker smoothed the coils together by tapping them with a wooden paddle. The details of the armor were carefully crafted onto the body with finer tools. Thin layers and strips of fresh clay were smoothed over the statue, then shaped into pants, folds in the clothing, and other details.

Heads and hands were created separately and attached to the bodies later. Some of the hands were shaped in molds, while others were crafted by hand. Most of the heads were made in molds, in two parts—one for the front half, the other for the back.

Giving each of the thousands of warriors its own individual character took astonishing skill and artistry. The potter coated the molded head with a half-inch-thick layer of fine clay and then sculpted the

In order to understand how the statues were made, modern Chinese potters do their best to reproduce the craft of their ancestors. Here a potter uses the coil method. ➤

Creating with Clay

Clay is an amazing material. When it is wet, it can be molded into just about any shape. When it dries, it keeps its shape but can be dissolved in water. If a clay object is fired, or baked at very high temperatures, it becomes hard and resistant to water. For thousands of years people have known about these useful properties of clay and have shaped it into all sorts of objects, from cups, bowls, and pitchers to tiles, bricks, and statues.

Terra-cotta is a common sort of hard-baked clay. The ancient Chinese weren't the only people to use it. Ancient Egyptians, Assyrians, Persians, and the early peoples of Central America all made terra-cotta pottery. The ancient Greeks were the first to use terra-cotta in architecture, shaping the clay into roof tiles and decorative details on buildings.

A worker carefully shapes the details of a head, using a photo of an original statue as a guide. ➤

features. Each face is not only unique but also very detailed. Young soldiers have round, smooth faces. Older warriors are leaner, with fine wrinkles. The eyes help create expressions that seem to show the personality of each warrior.

The statues were originally painted in bright colors. Using a computer, archaeologists can add the colors they think once decorated them.

Into the Fire

After the statues were shaped, they were left to dry in a room where they were protected from sunlight. Then they were fired, or baked, in a large oven called a kiln. Statues were fired for five days at high temperatures, from 1,652 to 1,832 degrees Fahrenheit (900 to 1,000 degrees Celsius).

Firing is a tricky process. Objects can crack or become deformed in the kiln. Modern sculptors who have tried to duplicate the work of the Qin potters have found that one out of ten of their firings is a failure.

Any one of several problems can ruin a statue. As it dries in the heat, the clay may shrink unevenly, pulling the statue out of shape. If the clay varies in thickness, firing may be uneven, causing the statue to crack. The clay in the emperor's warriors ranges in thickness from less than one inch to four inches (two to ten centimeters). The Qin potters solved this problem by cutting grooves, hollows, and holes where the clay was thick, so that the firing would be even all over.

After firing, the statues were removed from the kiln to cool. Then they were painted in bright colors: shades of red, green, blue, yellow, and brown, plus black and white.

Most of this paint did not survive the centuries underground. But from the bits that remain, scientists were able to learn about the chemistry of the paints used. They were surprised to find a purple pigment that they had thought was unknown in ancient China. At the time the warriors were created, most artists around the world used only paints made directly from nature, such as crushed minerals or vegetable dyes. But the Qin potters had figured out how to create their beautiful purple paint by combining minerals in a complex mixture that does not exist in nature.

The hope for life after death is expressed in this Chinese
painting from the Ming dynasty (A.D.1388–1644).
It illustrates the poem "Dreaming of Immortality in a
Thatched Cottage."

6

END OF A
DYNASTY

In 210 B.C. Qin Shihuangdi set out on one of
his journeys in search of immortality. He
visited parts of his empire along the Yangtze
River, then traveled along China's eastern
coast. The emperor had heard tales of a group
of magical islands in the eastern sea. The
islands were believed to be divine mountains
floating on the backs of giant turtles. The holy
men who lived there were said to hold the
secret of eternal life.

This was not the emperor's first
attempt to reach the blessed islands.
He had already sent expeditions
to find them and bring back
the elixir of life. But these
missions had failed.

When the searchers returned, they told the emperor that large fish had blocked their path. If only the fish could be killed, the emperor's search would be rewarded. Qin Shihuangdi decided to join the hunt himself. When he reached the coast, he saw several huge "fish" (probably whales) and killed one with his crossbow. Finally he seemed close to his goal. Then the emperor fell ill and died. He was forty-nine years old.

Final Journey

The officials journeying with the emperor didn't want anyone to know about his death. They were far from their stronghold, the capital city of Xianyang, and feared that news of Shihuangdi's death might start an uprising against the government. So they kept the death a secret. Placing the emperor's body in a carriage, they quickly set

Imperial Carriages

Until the 1980s historians had to be content with written descriptions of the luxurious carriages used by China's emperors. Then excavations near the First Emperor's tomb revealed a number of bronze models of magnificent carriages. Every detail of these horse-drawn wagons is beautifully cast, from the 440-pound (200-kilogram) horses to the tiny gold and silver decorations. The respected Chinese archaeologist Professor Su Bai calls them "the ultimate in bronze objects."

Each model is a wonderful miniature, half the size of one of Qin Shihuangdi's real carriages. Each has more than seven thousand precisely made parts, which were molded separately, then joined together in an exact fit. The carriages were richly decorated. They were painted in bright shades of red, pink, green, blue, and brown as well as white and black. Painted dragons, diamonds, clouds, and other designs covered the walls and doors. More than two thousand gold and silver ornaments adorn each miniature. The carriages are pulled by a team of four sturdy clay horses and driven by a lifelike coachman armed with a sword, bow, arrows, and a decorated shield.

Researchers believe that the carriages are exact copies of those used by the First Emperor. There are two designs. The inspection carriage is open to the air, to allow the emperor to get in and out easily while surveying his empire. The rest carriage is enclosed.

When Qin Shihuangdi toured his lands,

out for the capital, 600 miles (968 kilometers) to the west.

Only the most trusted officials accompanied the carriage on its sad journey. When the travelers halted for food along the way, meals were brought to the carriage as though the living emperor were inside. When local leaders asked to consult Shihuangdi about matters of government, the officials pretended to speak with the emperor, then made the decision themselves. As time passed, the emperor's body began to smell. The officials loaded a cart behind the carriage with rotting fish to disguise the odor. Finally the carriage arrived in Xianyang and the emperor's death was announced.

One of the emperor's sons, Huhai (hoo-hi), was declared the new ruler. Qin Shihuangdi was buried in the elaborate tomb that had been prepared for him. As the emperor had ordered before his death, many

A model of one of the emperor's rest carriages

he traveled in a caravan of carriages. On long journeys he brought along as many as eighty-one carriages, including roughly equal numbers of each design. After the emperor died unexpectedly during his final journey, his body was carried back to the capital in a rest carriage with curtains covering the windows.

of the craftspeople and laborers who had worked on the tomb complex were sealed in as well, so that they could not reveal its secrets. It is not known whether these unfortunate people were executed first or buried alive. A huge mound of earth was piled over the tomb and planted with bushes and trees, making it look like an ordinary mountain.

Qin Shihuangdi's dynasty did not last long after his death. Within a year rebels rose up against the second Qin emperor, who had continued his father's harsh policies. Work on the First Emperor's underground city halted, leaving Pit 4 empty and possibly other areas incomplete. In 206 B.C. the strongest of the rebel leaders took the throne as the first Han emperor. The Han dynasty lasted until A.D. 220. When it collapsed, China once again became a divided land. It would not be reunited for more than three hundred years.

Guardians for Eternity

During the battles that followed the First Emperor's death, the roof of Pit l was set afire. Parts of Pit 2 also burned, and the statues in Pit 3 were smashed. From time to time grave robbers stole some of the statues and weapons from the vaults. Eventually some of the roofing planks over the pits collapsed and the ground settled. The earth covering the pits came to look just like the surrounding plains, and knowledge of the existence of the terra-cotta army faded.

Through all these years of damage and neglect, Qin Shihuangdi's clay warriors stood helpless. Broken and buried in layers of earth, they seemed to have failed in the mission for which they were created. Then, more than two thousand years after the emperor's death, his terra-cotta army was accidentally rediscovered. In their unearthing, the warriors helped to ensure the First Emperor lasting fame, and a touch of the immortality he dreamed of when he built his fabulous eternal city.

Sifting, digging, measuring—workers continue to unearth China's incredible clay warriors. ➤

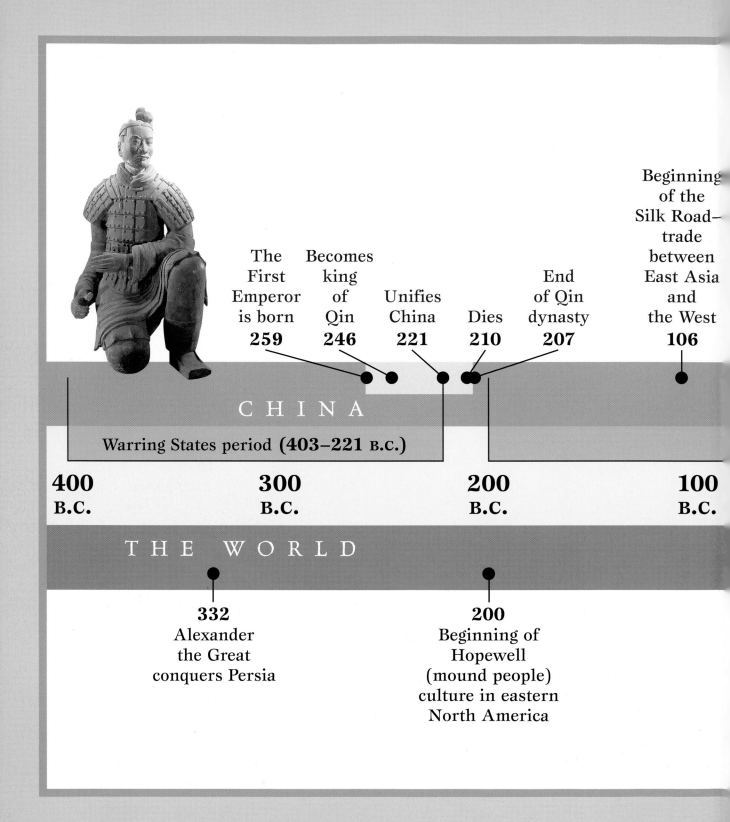

The
First
Emperor
is born
259

Becomes
king
of
Qin
246

Unifies
China
221

Dies
210

End
of Qin
dynasty
207

Beginning
of the
Silk Road–
trade
between
East Asia
and
the West
106

CHINA

Warring States period **(403–221 B.C.)**

400
B.C.

300
B.C.

200
B.C.

100
B.C.

THE WORLD

332
Alexander
the Great
conquers Persia

200
Beginning of
Hopewell
(mound people)
culture in eastern
North America

The Warriors in Time

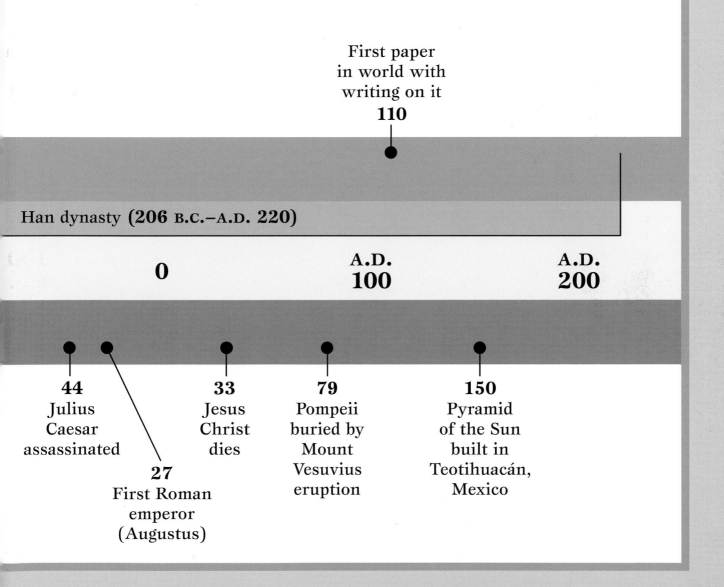

First paper
in world with
writing on it
110

Han dynasty **(206** B.C.–A.D. **220)**

0

A.D.
100

A.D.
200

44
Julius
Caesar
assassinated

27
First Roman
emperor
(Augustus)

33
Jesus
Christ
dies

79
Pompeii
buried by
Mount
Vesuvius
eruption

150
Pyramid
of the Sun
built in
Teotihuacán,
Mexico

Glossary

archaeologist: A scientist who studies tools, weapons, pottery, and other remains of ancient cultures to find out how people lived long ago.

artifact: An object made by people during a particular period of history.

cavalry: Soldiers who ride on horseback.

corrosion: The process of being weakened and eaten away gradually, as when metal rusts and wears away over time.

crossbow: A powerful weapon that has a bow mounted across a wooden stock. The stock has a groove to guide arrows and a notch to hold the bowstring when it is pulled back.

elixir of life: A magical potion that was believed to give the person who took it eternal life.

excavate: To uncover by digging.

immortality: Living, or lasting, forever.

infantry: Foot soldiers.

mace: A heavy club with a spiked metal head that was used as a weapon.

nomads: People who have no permanent home but instead wander from place to place, looking for food for themselves and their animals.

pi: A spear with a long shaft and double blades.

Qin Shihuangdi: The First Emperor of China. His name may be spelled other ways, including Qin Shi Huang, Ch'in Shih Huang, and Shi Huang Ti.

terra-cotta: A common kind of hard-baked clay used in many cultures for making statues, bowls, and other objects.

vault: An underground room or passage, or a safe storage compartment.

Xianyang: The capital of the Qin empire, located near where the city of Xi'an now lies.

For Further Reading

Books and Magazines

Cotterell, Arthur. *Ancient China*. Eyewitness Books Series. New York: Knopf, 1994.

Mazzatenta, O. Louis. "China's Warriors Rise from the Earth." *National Geographic*, October 1996, pp. 69–85.

Simpson, Judith. *Ancient China*. Nature Company Discoveries Series. Alexandria, VA: Time-Life Books, 1996.

Williams, Brian. *Ancient China*. See through History Series. New York: Viking, 1996.

*Websites**

http://www.whittier.edu/history/worldhist97/Qin/qin.htm This site offers some good information plus links to other sites.

http://www.npac.syr.edu/users/gcf/familyphotos/chinaterracotta/ There's no text but this site includes interesting images from the tomb.

*Websites change from time to time. For additional on-line information, check with the media specialist at your local library.

Bibliography

In addition to the following sources, some information comes from interviews with Zhang Tianzhu and Zhang Yinglan of the Archaeological Team at the Museum of Pottery Figures of Warriors and Horses from the Tomb of Qin Shihuangdi, Lintong, China, and from a video shown on the Discovery Channel entitled *The First Emperor*.

Fagan, Brian M., ed. *The Oxford Companion to Archaeology*. New York: Oxford University Press, 1996.

Fairbank, John King. *China: A New History*. Cambridge, MA: Harvard University Press, Belknap Press, 1992.

The First Emperor's Terracotta Legion. Beijing, China: China Travel and Tourism Press, 1988.

Huang, Ray. *China: A Macro History*. Armonk, NY: M. E. Sharpe, An East Gate Book, 1997.

Mazzatenta, O. Louis. "China's Warriors Rise from the Earth." *National Geographic*, October 1996, pp. 69–85.

Roberts, J. A. G. *A History of China*. Vol. 1, *Prehistory to c. 1800*. New York: St. Martin's Press, 1996.

Scarre, Chris. *Smithsonian Timelines of the Ancient World: A Visual Chronology from the Origins of Life to A.D. 1500*. New York: Dorling Kindersley, 1993.

Terra Cotta Warriors. Beijing, China: People's China Publishing House, 1997.

Tianchou, Fu, ed. *The Underground Terracotta Army of Emperor Qin Shihuangdi*. Beijing, China: New World Press, 1985.

Watson, Burton, trans. *Records of the Grand Historian: Qin Dynasty*. New York: Columbia University Press, 1993.

Index

Page numbers for illustrations are in **boldface**

About the Author

Dorothy Patent is the author of more than one hundred science and nature books for children and has won numerous awards for her writing. She has a Ph.D. in zoology from the University of California, Berkeley.

Although trained as a biologist, Dorothy has always been fascinated by the human past. At home, next to the books about animals, her shelves are jammed with titles such as *Mysteries of the Past.* When the opportunity came to write about other times and cultures for children, Dorothy plunged enthusiastically into the project. In the process of researching the FROZEN IN TIME series, she said, "I have had some great adventures and have come to understand much more deeply what it means to be human."

Dorothy lives in Missoula, Montana, with her husband, Greg, and their two dogs, Elsa and Ninja. They enjoy living close to nature in their home at the edge of a forest.